Prayers for the Journey

by

Barbara Mariconda

Illustrations by
Thomas Masaryk

Introduction
Prayers for the Journey

Inevitably, the journey of life will lead us through experiences of disappointment, sorrow, and loss. During these periods of suffering we can become blind to everyone and everything - except our own pain. The prayers in this volume can be your compass as you traverse your personal Path of Suffering, always pointing you toward the God who will be your strength, your hope, and your solace.

The volume is divided into six thematic sections:

The Path of Suffering
When the Ego Self Dominates
Moving Toward the Spirit Self
Mature Faith
Transformation of Self
Transformation of Others

Each prayer corresponds to a chapter from *"After the Diagnosis...A Guide for Living – The Transformative Power of Love During Sickness, Dying, and Death."* You can read each prayer before beginning the chapter, and as you work your way through it, perhaps morning and evening to bring greater resonance of the material into your own situation. Or, you might carry this slender book with you each day, turning to whichever prayer calls to your heart. Doing so will help you surrender to something greater than yourself, something larger than your distress, and bigger than your fear – and that something is God. You might also meditate on the evocative illustrations by artist Thomas Masaryk, allowing your soul to take from them whatever it needs.

Together, may the prayers and illustrations be a balm for your spirit, a light along your path, revealing to you in a much greater way, the working of God in your life.

Section 1

The Path
of
Suffering

At some point in time – and, likely more than once, each of us will find ourselves faced with something we'd rather not have to deal with. It might be some significant loss - of a relationship, a job, a home, some part of our identity, our health. All of these losses threaten our sense of security, safety, and sense of self, and ultimately put us on "The Path of Suffering." We struggle through a painfully predictable and, at the same time, uniquely individual set of responses and emotions that leave us anxious and self-absorbed. During these times we desperately need a guide to lead us safely along this path…we can't do it on our own strength. And that guide is God.

The three prayers that follow will validate your experience and help you to connect with God, our comfort and our strength.

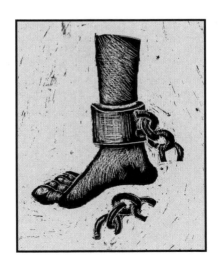

✝

My God...
When my life changes in an instant,
When I'm confronted with the reality of tragedy,
the ruthlessness of death,
let me know the safety of your arms through
the open, honest, and loving care
of those around me.
Grant me the faith and confidence
to pass from this phase of the Journey to the next,
whenever my day shall come,
empowered with your courage, grace, and peace.
AMEN

✝

Dear Lord...
I find myself on a difficult path
that I prefer not to travel.
Let me never forget that you are my
constant companion, my loving guide.
When I'm afraid, Lord, reassure me.
When in pain, comfort me.
When I grow weak, be my strength.
When discouraged, give me hope.
When I fall, Lord, pick me up.
When alone, be my solace.
When I lose faith,
Restore me.
AMEN

My God...
Help me to know who I am in you alone.
Grant me the courage to remove the ego mask,
to put aside all unreality that holds me captive.
Relieve me of the need to cling tightly,
to grasp and control, to compare and to judge.
Lead me, Lord, to become more of
a human being, less of a human mindlessly doing—
so that in coming back to myself
I may find you there.
AMEN

Section 2

When the
Ego Self
Dominates

All of us are creatures of the culture. We learn, from the moment of our births, what the culture expects from us. We're rewarded when we respond accordingly, and we're marginalized when we don't. In time, we forget who we were really born to be – children of the living God. We embrace and nurture the persona crafted by the culture and begin to believe that these masks we wear are really who we are. When faced with adversity we turn to the culture for help – we may try to deny the seriousness of the situation, or turn to other children of the culture to help us. When that fails, we turn to our faith, which, when filtered through the culture, is shallow and weak. When this happens, it feels as though we've been let down by everyone and everything we believed in. We find ourselves in a prison of our own making...

Pray the following five prayers when worldly support systems have let you down, when what you need is the loving mercy of the counter-cultural God who has the power to save us...

Jesus my Lord...
You said that you were in the world
but not of the world.
Help me to know your ways,
To stand in the tension between
this world and the next.
Give me the eyes to see, the ears to hear.
A discerning heart, and willing spirit
to traverse the way of freedom and love—
to be in this world, but not of it.
AMEN

My God...

It is difficult to face the reality before me.

Open my eyes to accept the road ahead.

Lord, be my shield. Defend me from harm.

Be my unfailing strength in times of challenge.

Help me to deal with "what is..."

And with your help, to embrace this cross,

and follow in your footsteps.

AMEN

My God...
There are times when those I need the most
let me down.
Lord, in those moments, be for me
my mother, my father, my sister, my brother.
Stand by me as devoted spouse,
care for me as beloved son, as devoted daughter.
In this way, may my expectations
never call another up short,
for you, Lord, are my portion and my cup.

AMEN

Oh Lord,

There are times when my faith is so weak.

I place before you my doubts and fears,

my years of neglect, the sense of being far from you.

I offer up my anger, my tendency to bargain and beg.

Help me trust that this admission is but a first

tentative step

toward a broader faith, a faith large enough

to hold my every human weakness.

AMEN

Sweet Jesus...
You said, "I have come to set captives free..."
Lord, I long for this freedom, to stand unfettered
from the confines of my mind.
Free me from the chains of anxiety that hold me in bondage,
from past regrets and future fears.
Liberate me from "Why?" and "Why not?"
Help me to stand in the gift of this present moment,
fully alive, with you by my side.
AMEN

Section 3

Moving Toward the Spirit Self

Human beings, by nature, are resistant to change. Yet without change, growth is impossible. The question is, does the situation you're in hurt enough to propel you to respond to life differently? In order to tip the fulcrum of our lives away from the constraints of the ego and toward the freedom of the spirit requires a new lens, a new way of seeing, a new way of walking the path. The old ways must be dismantled in order to lay ourselves bare, embracing our brokenness, our vulnerabilities and losses - even our own mortality. To move to this uncharted territory requires confidence – not in ourselves, but in the loving and merciful God who dwells within us.

Read and reflect on the following six prayers whenever you are trying to rally the strength to change. To grow. To break out of the chains that hold us bound and prevent us from living fully.

My God...

I stand before you carefully guarded,

Burying my vulnerability, hiding my losses,

pushing away any hint of mortality.

Uncover me, O Lord!

Let me bare my soul to you

so that I can embrace my own brokenness,

ready and willing to be put together again

in your image.

AMEN

O, Sweet Jesus...
I do not want to walk this path —
but here I am, Lord.
Will you walk beside me?
You thoroughly know the way.
Guide me to follow in your footsteps,
that I, too, may accept the help
of those along the road,
forgiving life and others
so as to lighten the cross I bear.
May the way of suffering
illuminate for me your way of love.
AMEN

My God...

Whenever I long for you, remind me to look within.

Help me to see past the disguise of the ego and

the shroud of sin.

Let me believe, Lord,

that we are all inherently good,

that beneath our neediness, our brokenness,

and our weakness, there you are.

Give me eyes to see myself and others

as you see us.

Turn us inside out, Lord,

so we can be your face for the world.

AMEN

✝

My Lord and my God...
Teach me how to see with eyes of love.
As I'm emptied by life,
hollowed by suffering,
diminished by pain,
reduced through loss,
let me see what remains as pure love...as your love.
At the end of my days, may I bathe myself in this love
and let it overflow into the world I leave behind.
AMEN

O God...
Who are you, really?
Do you love me, Lord? Is it true?
Open my eyes and reveal yourself to me!
Not as a distant figure, but as a friend,
Not a far-off deity, but a confidante.
As I reach for you, stretch your arms my way,
reminding me that as I show love to others,
I'll know love from you.

AMEN

O Sweet Jesus,
Help me to remember
that everyone has a story,
That life bruises all of us
in ways seen and unseen.
Grant me, O Lord, a compassionate heart,
And eyes of mercy that look only for good.
Water the seeds of the fertile patch in all of us.
And help me to do the same.

AMEN

Section 4

Mature Faith

For most of us, it doesn't take very long to experience the brokenness of life, the randomness of loss, and the pain of suffering. As time unfolds we're forced to let go of our expectations and reevaluate all that we took for granted. Adjusting to the life we find ourselves living can result in maturity and growth, or in bitterness and resentment. Our grade-school faith no longer sustains us, and we turn to spiritual practices that produce the dispositions of mature faith, providing the grace we need to let go of everything that is no longer life-giving. When life empties us, we begin to stand with open arms before our God, waiting to be filled, so that we, in turn, can spill that sacred love into the fields of our lives.

These next five prayers help us to embrace the art of surrender, and to engage in the discipline of spiritual practices that yield the harvest of a more seasoned, realistic faith.

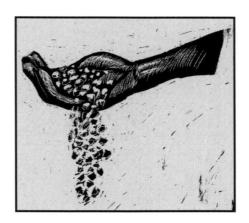

O God...
My faith is messy.
I offer it to you humbly, just as it is.
Accept it, O Lord, as an evolving gift
that I present again and again,
knowing that each time I raise my arms to you
you reach back with an embrace.
And when I forget, as I surely will,
when I flail and fall,
Help me get up again and
move once more toward you.
AMEN

✝

O God of Peace,

Help me to strip away all of the distractions

that cloud my awareness of you.

How I cling to the noise and the clutter around me!

Settle my anxious thoughts, O Lord.

Slow my incessant striving.

Silence the inner voices.

Soothe my needy soul

that I may rest in your presence,

at peace, at one with you alone.

AMEN

✝

O God of Love...
To you I offer my morning,
this day of mine, and evening,
precious in its ordinariness.
Let my life be my prayer, my sacrifice.
Help me mark the hours with small acts of
awareness, intention, and practice,
honing, ever honing,
a heart open to you, O Lord...
One moment,
one hour,
one day at a time.
AMEN

✝

O God...
Help me see what it is besides you
that I worship and adore
and recognize why it fails to satisfy.
Let me instead turn with hands upraised,
and voice in song,
face upturned in awe of the mystery that is you.
May I join with all and worship well,
lose myself as words and gestures flow,
as they have throughout the ages.
May I be a thread in the tapestry of this rich tradition,
woven one with all in you.
AMEN

✝

O God of Love...
Let me never lose sight of your mercy.
Make me a vessel for your love,
a channel through which compassion and
understanding flow.
In this way may I love at ever-higher levels,
Not through my efforts,
but in and through you.
And, Lord, in my final days,
may I traverse the spiral of love
that leads all to you.
AMEN

Section 5

Transformation of Self...

Relying on God's Love

How, in the midst of life's challenges, can we begin to evolve into more spiritual beings? Into people who view life through the lens of love and act out of that love? As much as this may seem to involve an inward movement, it's actually an outward thrust that begins to transform us. In doing little things with great love, by committing to forgiveness and healing, by allowing ourselves to be vulnerable with others in sharing not only the stories of our lives, but our spiritual journeys – this is how we begin to lay our self interest aside in order to be for others. In doing so, we ourselves are transformed. As we hear in 1 John, "Those who love know God."

These next four prayers can open your hearts to the strength and courage you need to reach out in this way. Doing so is an entre into the transformation of self that begins and ends with love.

✝

Loving God...

Help me today to be totally present

to those around me.

Lead me from myself, Lord,

from my self-absorption and pain

so that I can be for another.

When I'm afraid or suffering,

help me to reach out with a kind word,

gesture, or smile.

I may not be capable of great things, Lord...

But help me, day by day,

to extend myself by doing the smallest

things with great love.

AMEN

✝

Merciful God...

Help me to experience your forgiveness,

so that in knowing your compassion

I might extend it to others.

Heal my wounds, Lord,

ease the sting of each offense.

Restore my dignity, so, whole again,

I may forgive the hurts inflicted on me by others.

Whether reconciled or not,

may I sow peace, seek understanding,

knowing that those who cause me pain

do so out of wounds of their own.

Heal these unending circles of hurt, Lord,

and give me the courage to do my part.

AMEN

O Lord,

expand the fertile field of my heart.

As I become more aware of your presence,

may I come to see my own story

through eyes of compassion.

Help me to embrace the whole of it —

to recognize the joys and pain, triumphs and failures.

as parts of a sacred story

that begins and ends with you.

May I own my story, and in doing so

experience the holiness of sharing it with another.

AMEN

Holy Spirit...
lead me to someone with whom I can
travel the spiritual journey.
Someone who will listen with an open heart,
and challenge me to grow in faith,
May my soul partner bring God to me,
and me to God.
And may I do the same.
AMEN

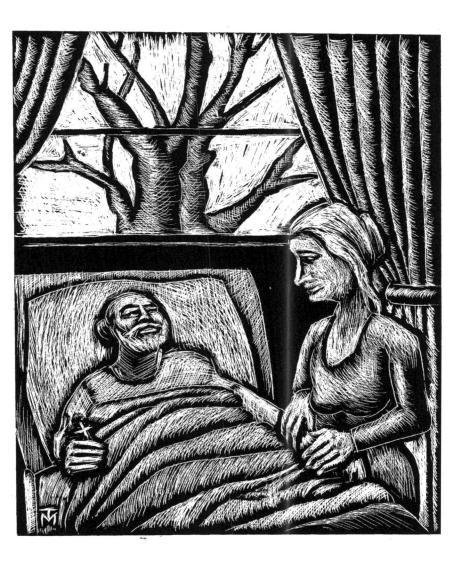

Section 6

Transformation of Others

The transformation of others in our lives and in the world requires an alchemy of vulnerability, compassion, and love. The process is not so much dependent upon us, but on our willingness to allow the love of God to flow through, to warm the climate of our relationships, to inform our conversations, and to give us the grace to hear and understand the stories of others. When we begin to really own ourselves, to embrace our struggles and weaknesses, we open the doors of our hearts and invite others in. And when we're suffering and relationally depleted, and somehow take the leap of faith required in letting go, God's love will carry us and overflow to others. The passion and purity of this love has the power to transform and heal.

These final nine prayers are meant to oil the hinges on the doors of our hearts that we might prefer not to open. But, throwing them ajar can change everything.

✝

My God...
There is so much I long to say...
so much I need to hear.
But where to begin?
May your Spirit warm the climate
so words may flow from my heart
to the heart of another.
Guide our talk, Lord, so that our every exchange
may bring freedom and light,
healing and love.
AMEN

Loving God,

Open my eyes and my heart

to see and acknowledge that which must be said.

Lead me and those I love

to a place where we can be vulnerable together...

to a place where difficult words may unlock

feelings unspoken.

Open the channels of love, Lord,

and place the words on my tongue

that will heal and enlighten.

AMEN

My Compassionate God...
Give me the courage to face my fears,
and speak them aloud,
and the patience to listen and to hear.
Help me to know another
by revealing my deepest self,
trusting that intimacy is born of sharing.
Lord, prepare the heart of my confidante,
to hold my vulnerability like a fragile gift.
Guide our every exchange,
and set our words apart as holy.
AMEN

My God...
As emotions run high
there is little energy left for practical things.
Give me the strength to take on one task at a time
and to acknowledge each as an expression of love.
Help me to simplify my life,
to remove the clutter of anything
that steals my attention
from that which is most important.
AMEN

Most Loving God...
There are some decisions
that just seem too difficult to make.
Stand beside me, Lord,
and give me the courage to face these choices
with deep trust and hope in you.
Take my hand and lead me toward clarity.
Help me to take responsibility for my care
so that those I love will be spared painful choices.
AMEN

O God...
Why is it that we sometimes
avoid the words we most need to say?
Grant me a well-trained tongue, Lord.
May my words soar like a free bird,
lifting sacred sentiments to life
through messages of love...
Thank you.
I love you.
Farewell.
AMEN

O God of Life...
As we stand at the threshold
between this world and the next,
bless us with the peace that comes
from confidence in all you promise.
Cradle us in joyful hope, surrounded by those
who are your hands and heart in this world.
Help us to gratefully surrender all,
and gently take our leave.
Whole again, may we run to you
and gaze upon you, finally,
face to face.
AMEN

✝

Merciful God...
When death occurs,
those left in its wake are bereft, lost.
May the age-old rites of passage
provide healing and hope,
that the Word of God be a balm of solace
to fill the empty spaces in our hearts.
Grant that all who come together
may pray well,
that their souls be lifted by song,
and that they leave the grave
with greater hope and faith,
infused with the love of the departed.
AMEN

✝

O God of Compassion...

You promise to wipe away every tear from our eyes.

But when grief comes, it sets up house and stays.

Help us, Lord, to welcome this dark visitor,

to embrace this shadow-side of love.

Let us recall the gifts,

savor the richness of what was

as we cast open the windows of the present

to let in the sun.

May we look to the future with hope,

and move through each day

strengthened by the one love inside

that is both God and our beloved.

AMEN

Related books by Barbara Mariconda (with coauthor Fr. Thomas F. Lynch)

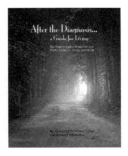

After the Diagnosis...A Guide for Living... *The Transformative Power of Love During Sickness, Dying, and Death* (Available on our website: www.journeyofthesoulbooks.com, on Amazon, and by special order at your local bookstore.)

Reflections on the Journey – A companion journal of reflection questions to use alone, with a Soul Partner, or in small group discussions. (Available on our website: www.journeyofthesoulbooks.com)

Reach the authors at www.journeyofthesoulbooks.com CONTACT US for information regarding talks, retreats, and presentations, as well as discounts on bulk orders of 25 or more books.

For daily support and inspiration, JOIN our Journey of the Soul Community on Facebook: https://www.facebook.com/groups/2036967826563303/

Made in the USA
Columbia, SC
04 March 2020